Fragile Earth

Contents

Changing Earth	2
Earthquakes	4
Volcanoes	10
Extreme weather	14
The power of water	22
Human impact	30
Global warming	40
Observing the Earth	50
Glossary	52
Index	53
Review	54

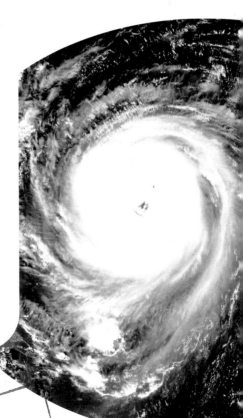

Written by Claire Llewellyn

Changing Earth

The Earth is always changing. We may not notice it from day to day, but small changes are constantly taking place on the Earth's surface. Mountains slowly wear away, valleys grow deeper and cliffs crumble into the sea. Meanwhile, oceans freeze and thaw, lakes shrink and rivers change their course. Why? Because forces are acting upon the Earth. Some of these are natural forces and are beyond our control; others are the work of people. All of these forces cause change.

Natural changes

Some of the most powerful forces that affect our planet take place under the Earth's surface. Here, hot, **molten** rock, which is gently moving, can cause devastating earthquakes and volcanoes. Meanwhile, above our heads, other forces are at work. As the Sun heats the air around us, it creates the winds that bring our weather. Violent storms batter coasts, while rain and snow send flood water pouring over the land. Rivers also change the landscape, wearing away rock into tiny pieces, which build up further downstream.

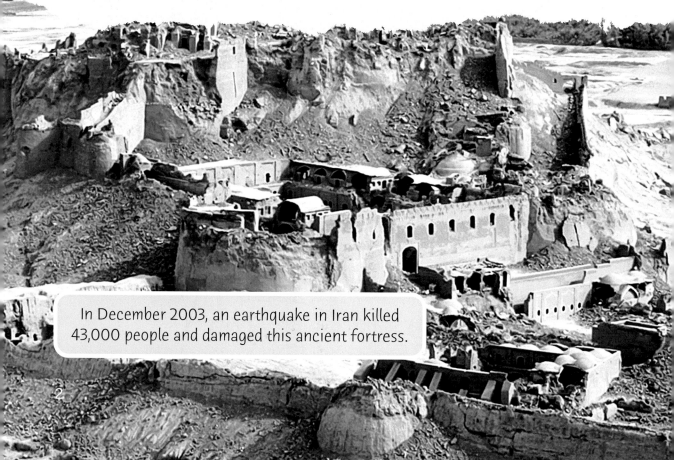

In December 2003, an earthquake in Iran killed 43,000 people and damaged this ancient fortress.

Human changes

Humans change the landscape too. We clear forests to make room for buildings and farms. We mine and quarry the land for useful materials. We take water from rivers to irrigate farms. Some of our actions are causing environmental problems. One of these is global warming, which is resulting in rising sea levels and more extreme weather. These, in turn, cause further change.

New Orleans suffered widespread flooding after a hurricane hit the city in October 2005.

open-cast mining at Carajas, Brazil, one of the world's largest mines

Observing change

This book examines some of the ways in which our world is changing. Many of the photographs included here have been taken from **satellites**, high above the Earth (for more about this, see pages 50–51). Photos of the same area, taken several years apart, can reveal dramatic changes. Some of the photos show how we're harming the Earth. These pictures are very valuable, because only when we understand the results of our actions can we do something about them.

Earthquakes

The Earth's crust

Planet Earth is a rocky ball. Around the outside of the planet is a hard layer
between five and 60 kilometres thick. This layer is called the crust and it covers the
entire planet. It lies beneath the seas and oceans, as well as beneath the continents –
the seven vast land masses found on the Earth.

The crust resembles the peel that covers a fruit. However, unlike the peel, the Earth's
crust is broken. It has cracked into sections, called plates, which fit together around
the globe like the pieces of a giant jigsaw. There are seven large plates and about
a dozen smaller ones.
Each plate has been
given a name. For
example, the plate
that lies below
the Indian Ocean,
the continent of
Oceania and the
Indian Sub-Continent
is known as the
Indo-Australian Plate.

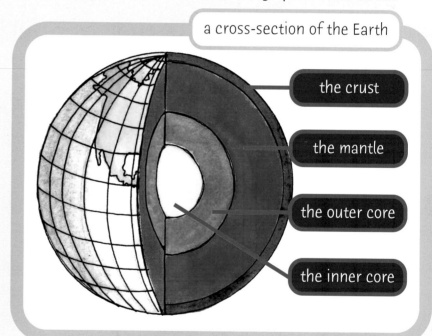

a cross-section of the Earth

the crust

the mantle

the outer core

the inner core

Under the surface

Below the Earth's rocky crust lies another, thicker layer called the mantle. Nearly
3,000 kilometres thick, the mantle is also made of rock, but because temperatures
here are very hot some of the rock has melted. The hard plates drift on this molten
rock, like rafts on a syrupy sea, with some plates moving up to 20 centimetres per
year. At the places where two plates meet, the huge slabs of rock can grind together
or pull apart. This has dramatic results that cause earthquakes and volcanoes.

Earthquakes

Earthquakes are often caused when plates that have been jammed together for centuries suddenly lurch, jerking themselves free. The sudden shift sends out huge shock waves, known as seismic waves, which cause the surface of the Earth to shake. Earthquakes are fairly common; in fact, many can occur on a single day and be relatively harmless. However, a major earthquake is very destructive. In minutes, it can cause landslides, shatter villages and towns, and bring buildings crashing to the ground.

Fact box:

The Mercalli scale measures the strength of an earthquake. It is made up of 12 points, for example:

Point 1: gentle tremor, detected only by scientific instruments

Point 4: loose objects move

Point 6: windows break, chimney pots fall down

Point 9: houses collapse, water and gas pipes crack

Point 12: ground ripples, total destruction of buildings

Tsunamis

Many earthquakes occur under the sea. They're barely noticeable there, but the seismic waves travel outwards towards land at hundreds of kilometres an hour. As they reach shallow water near the shore, the seismic waves slow down but build into a huge wave of water known by the Japanese name of tsunami. Tsunamis can be up to 75 metres high and are highly destructive, smashing harbours and drowning islands. A tsunami that occurred in the Indian Ocean in December 2004 killed more than 220,000 people.

a satellite image of Kalutara, Sri Lanka, shortly after the tsunami struck on 26 December 2004

5

Kobe, Japan, January 1995: a major earthquake struck early in the morning. It destroyed buildings and roads and killed 5,500 people.

Kobe, Japan, 2002: roads and buildings have been rebuilt. They are designed to be quake-proof.

A coach hangs over the collapsed expressway. An earthquake may last only seconds, but can still cause tremendous damage.

Tsunami devastation

Banda Aceh, Sumatra, Indonesia, 2003: the edge of the town can be seen top right in this satellite picture. Close by, there are woods and areas of farmland.

Banda Aceh, Sumatra, Indonesia, December 2004: an earthquake under the Indian Ocean sent a powerful tsunami racing to the shore. It destroyed buildings, stripped vegetation from the ground and left farmland under water.

Volcanoes

There are many thousands of volcanoes on the Earth. Some of them are found on land, but many of them lie on the seabed and erupt into the ocean. Volcanoes are particularly common around the shores of the Pacific Ocean, which is sometimes known as "the ring of fire". It's a region where some of the Earth's plates meet, causing volcanoes as they collide. Every year, all over the world, there are thousands of volcanic eruptions.

What causes an eruption?

A volcano starts in the Earth's mantle. Here, the molten rock, which is known as magma, rises and collects in a chamber below a weak spot in the Earth's crust. Gas and water mix with the magma, creating an explosive brew. Gradually, the pressure builds up (like a can of fizzy drink when it's shaken) until the magma, along with gas, steam and ash, are forced upwards and blast through the Earth's crust.

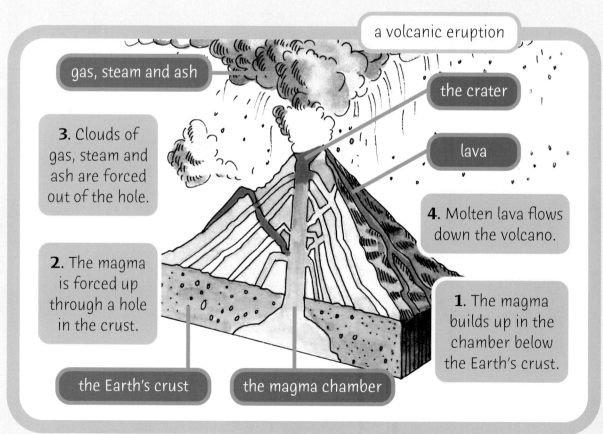

a volcanic eruption

gas, steam and ash

the crater

lava

3. Clouds of gas, steam and ash are forced out of the hole.

4. Molten lava flows down the volcano.

2. The magma is forced up through a hole in the crust.

1. The magma builds up in the chamber below the Earth's crust.

the Earth's crust

the magma chamber

Violent eruptions

Some eruptions are very violent. The molten rock, now known as lava, sprays out like a fountain of fire, while huge clouds of gas and ash shoot into the sky. Nearby towns may be overwhelmed by poisonous gases, falling ash and burning flows of lava. The lava flows downhill, burning and destroying everything in its path.

From 1963–65, volcanic eruptions under the North Atlantic Ocean caused lava to build up from the ocean floor. This resulted in a new island for Iceland. It was named Surtsey.

Volcanologist Christina Heliker is taking a sample of lava during an eruption of Kilauea Volcano, Hawaii.

Changing the landscape

In time, the hot lava cools and hardens. With each eruption, the lava builds higher until it forms a broad, low mound or a cone-shaped mountain. Parts of the mountain may themselves be destroyed in future eruptions. Although the surrounding land suffers after an eruption, the effects are not all bad. Volcanic ash and rock are rich in **minerals**, which help to fertilise the soil. In fact, the land around a volcano is some of the most fertile in the world.

Active or extinct?

Scientists place volcanoes in three different groups: active, dormant or extinct. Active volcanoes may erupt at any time. They are closely monitored by experts, known as volcanologists, who try to predict when they are likely to erupt. Dormant volcanoes have not erupted for centuries, but may do so in the future. Extinct volcanoes, as their name suggests, are no longer likely to erupt.

A sudden volcanic eruption

Mount St Helens, Washington, USA, May 1980: following 123 years of inactivity, the volcano awoke, triggered by earthquakes in the area. The cloud of ash towered 25 kilometres into the sky.

Before the eruption: Mount St Helens was a cone-shaped volcano. It was surrounded by large forests that were home to elk, bear and other wildlife.

After the eruption: the north face of the mountain collapsed. A wall of ash, steam, water and mud raced outwards, felling trees and killing wildlife over a huge area. Fifty-seven people lost their lives.

Extreme weather

The world's weather is always changing. Winds blow in different weather conditions – wet or windy, dry or calm. In many parts of the world, the seasons alter the weather too. Fine summers are replaced by colder, wetter weather and in winter there may be snow. In all parts of the world, now and again, the weather may become extreme. Violent storms, such as hurricanes and tornadoes, can batter and devastate the land.

Hurricanes

Hurricanes are dangerous tropical storms, which start over the ocean in the warmest season, when sea temperatures are at least 24 degrees centigrade. Hot, steamy air rises quickly from the water, forming thick clouds that start to spin. Day by day, the storm grows bigger. As the clouds tower higher, the winds spin faster and suck up more moist air from the sea, which feeds the growing storm. A hurricane can be hundreds of kilometres wide, with winds whirling at up to 300 kilometres per hour around a calm centre known as the eye. Once formed, the storm moves slowly across the ocean towards the land.

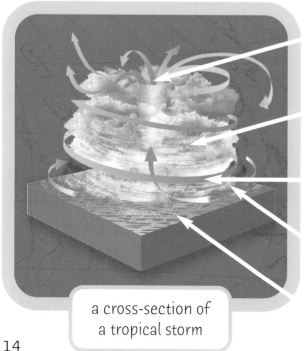

The eye is a calm area, up to 50 kilometres wide, in the very centre of the storm.

bands of rain

Whirling winds reach speeds of up to 300 kilometres per hour.

Moist air is sucked up and feeds the storm.

a cross-section of a tropical storm

warm sea

Storm damage

When a hurricane hits the coast, huge storm waves **surge** towards the shore, destroying harbours and causing flooding. Heavy rain and ferocious winds flatten buildings, uproot trees and destroy crops. Because a hurricane is so large, it may take 18 hours for the storm to pass over. Little by little, it blows itself out, because, when passing over land instead of sea, there is no damp air to feed it. Hurricanes occur throughout the tropics. They're called cyclones in India, typhoons in the Far East and willy-willies in Australia.

Tornadoes

Tornadoes, sometimes known as "twisters", are smaller than hurricanes. They form when a column of air sinks down from a thundercloud and warm air rises around it. As the air spirals upwards, it sucks up dirt from the ground, forming a tall, dark funnel. If the tornado forms over water, the whirling air sucks up water instead and is known as a waterspout. Tornadoes are about 100 metres wide and last for less than an hour. However, the winds whirl round at up to 450 kilometres per hour – much faster than a hurricane – and can demolish buildings or suck up trains. These storms can happen anywhere, but the United States of America suffers from more tornadoes than any other country.

Tropical storms are easily seen from space. This satellite picture shows the large, spiralling clouds of a typhoon over the China Sea.

After Hurricane Katrina

This satellite picture shows an area of New Orleans, where a canal has been cut to the Mississippi River.

In August 2005, heavy rain and a nine-metre surge from the sea poured over the flood defences, leaving much of the city under water.

As flood water poured into New Orleans, streets and pavements disappeared, parked cars were almost **submerged** and palm trees were uprooted.

Long and grey like an elephant's trunk, a tornado formed over the coast of Croatia in July 2004.

A tornado picks up all kinds of **debris** and swirls it through the air.

A tornado's track is often very narrow. Some houses here have been completely destroyed, while others have been hardly touched.

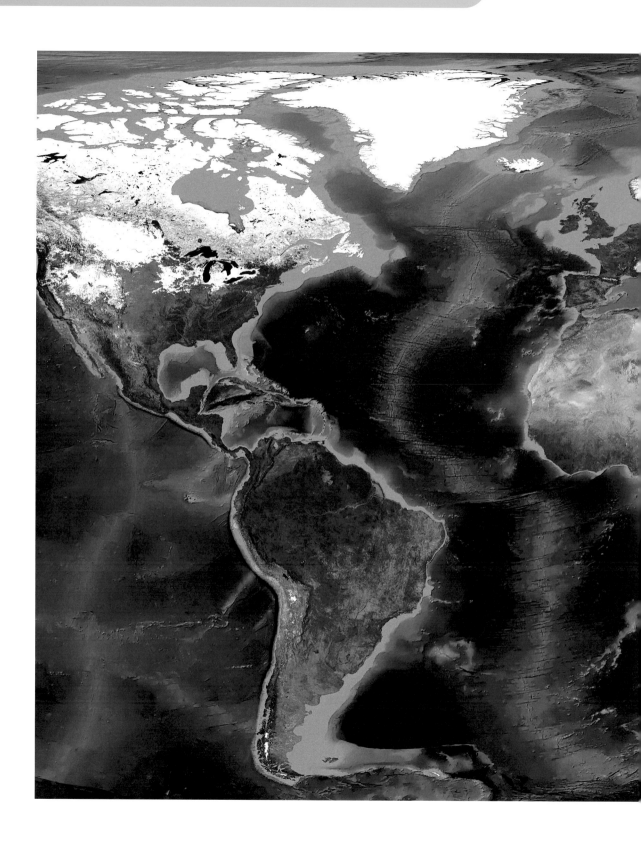

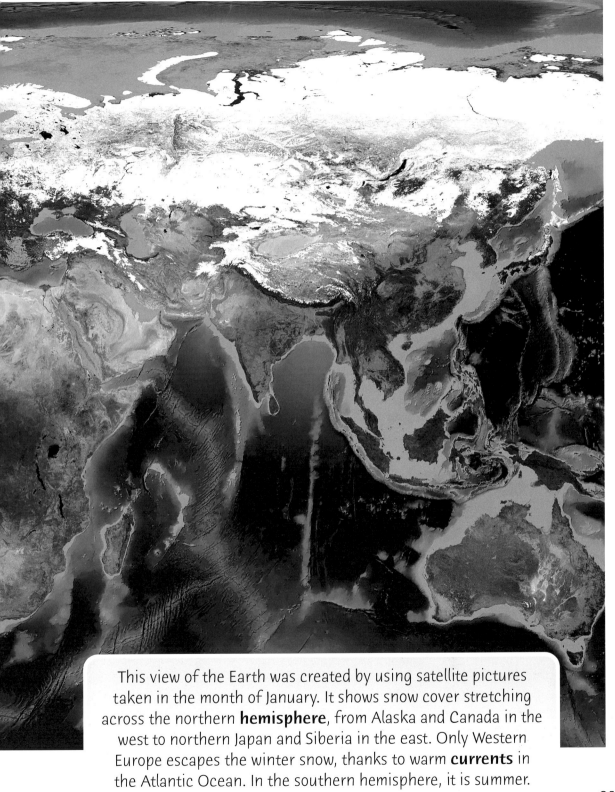

This view of the Earth was created by using satellite pictures taken in the month of January. It shows snow cover stretching across the northern **hemisphere**, from Alaska and Canada in the west to northern Japan and Siberia in the east. Only Western Europe escapes the winter snow, thanks to warm **currents** in the Atlantic Ocean. In the southern hemisphere, it is summer.

The power of water

Moving water is a powerful force that can change the landscape in dramatic ways. Pounding waves and rushing rivers wear the land away in a process called erosion. They can also flood the land and cause widespread destruction. Yet water can also create new land, for example when a river dumps mud and stone and builds a fertile delta.

Waves at work

The sea endlessly **erodes** the land. As the tides roll in and out and waves pound the shore, pebbles are hurled against the cliffs. The cliffs slowly begin to crumble – first into boulders, then into pebbles, then into shingle and finally into sand. Coastlines are made of different kinds of rock. Cliffs that are made of mud and clay are easily eroded. As the waves nibble deeper and deeper, the shoreline gradually moves inland, with the result that places that were once safe from the sea soon feel the force of the waves.

Norfolk, UK, 2001

Norfolk, UK, 2005: this coastline has been so eroded that, in just four years, several buildings have fallen into the sea. The house in the square is now at risk.

Rivers

Rivers also erode the land. A fast-flowing stream carries stones along that scour
the river bed and carve out valleys. Meanwhile, tiny grains of sand and mud float
along in the water. The river grows wider on flatter ground, as many side streams
join it. After periods of heavy rain, the river may swell and burst its banks, causing
widespread flooding. Flooding is relatively harmless if the land is covered by natural
vegetation – in fact, it helps to fertilise the soil. However, as more land is used for
farming or building, floods can cause huge damage and even loss of life.

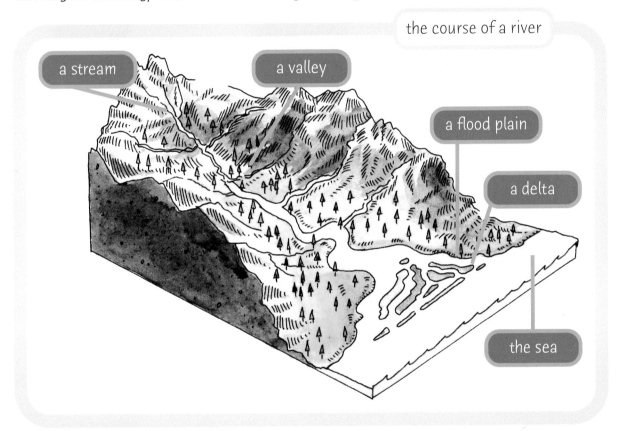

the course of a river

a stream

a valley

a flood plain

a delta

the sea

Building a delta

Rivers may sometimes be destructive but they can also create new land. As a river
flows towards the sea, it carries huge amounts of mud and sand. When the river
meets the sea, the mud and sand sink to the bottom and start to build up at the
mouth of the river. In some rivers, there is so much mud that the water is forced
to flow around it. Gradually, the mud builds higher, dries out and creates a delta –
an area of flat, fertile land at the river's mouth.

Cape Hatteras, North Carolina, USA, 1999:
beach houses and small hotels stand on the shore
of this small island off the Atlantic coast.

Cape Hatteras, North Carolina, USA, 2004:
after five years of coastal erosion, the shoreline has
moved, leaving this and other houses close to destruction.

St Louis, Missouri, USA, August 1991: this satellite image shows an area near St Louis where three rivers – the Mississippi, Missouri and Illinois – all meet. Most of the land along the banks, once covered by natural vegetation, is now used for farming.

St Louis, Missouri, USA, August 1993: after a long period of wet weather, all three rivers have broken their banks, flooding nearby farmland. The red areas in this picture show the stripped, bare soil that is left behind as flood water drains away.

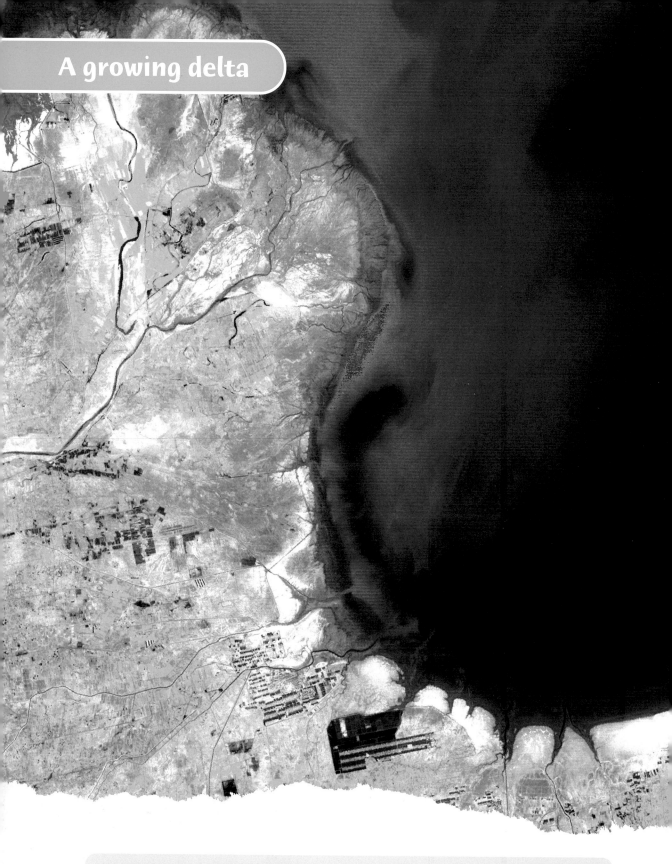

A growing delta

Yellow River, China, 1979: this satellite picture shows where the muddy Yellow River flows into the sea. As the river's current slows, fine grains of mud sink to the bottom and build a delta at the river's mouth.

Yellow River, China, 2000: 21 years later, the delta has grown.

Human impact

The Earth is billions of years old. If this vast period of time was represented as a single day, humans would have been around for less than one second. Yet, in that brief time, we've had a huge impact on the planet and our growing population is causing a number of environmental problems.

The human population

The world's human population is growing fast. From six billion in the year 2000, it's expected to reach ten billion by the end of the 21st century. Half of us live in vast, crowded cities, which gobble up more and more of the surrounding land. Our need for more homes, water, fuel and food is always increasing. This is placing a great strain on the Earth's limited **resources**.

From forests to farms

All over the world, land that was once wild is now being used to cultivate food. Vast areas of tropical rainforests are being cleared to make room for plantations to grow foods like palm oil and soya beans. Rainforests are very important. They are home to around half of the world's plant and animal species, which depend on them for life. The forests are vital in other ways too – they produce oxygen for us to breathe; they circulate water around the planet; and their roots help to bind the soil and protect it from blowing and washing away in the wind and rain.

an orang-utan mother and baby

What about water?

Water is another precious resource. We need water to grow crops and yet, sometimes, rains fail and rivers run dry. Many rivers have now been dammed, as we try to control the water supply. A dam creates a vast **reservoir** of water, which prevents flooding further downstream. In deserts, where there are few rivers, water that collects under the ground is used to irrigate farmland. This provides local people with food, but the "greening" of the desert may cause problems in the future because more groundwater is being used than can be replaced by rain.

The Hoover Dam was built across the Colorado River to control flooding and supply water for drinking and **irrigation** in the hot, dry state of Nevada.

Repairing the damage

We take many good things out of the Earth. Sometimes it seems that we put back only harmful things like waste and pollution. However, we often change landscapes for the better by restoring them to their natural state. For example, by planting trees throughout the tropics we can gradually replace the forests we've plundered. We can repair the damage we've caused.

Nobel Prize winner Wangari Maathai is planting a tree. In 1977 she founded the Green Belt Movement, which has now planted over 30 million trees across Kenya to prevent soil erosion.

Expanding cities

Hong Kong harbour, 1920: traditional **junks** shelter in the harbour.
In the background the hills are mostly bare.

Hong Kong harbour, 2000: the harbour is now surrounded by fast roads and high-rise apartment blocks. These house the growing population on small plots of land.

Deforestation

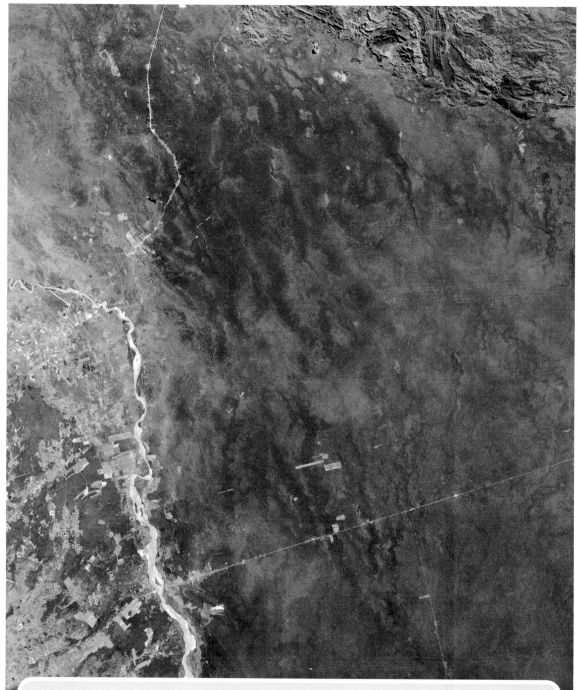

Near Santa Cruz, Bolivia, 1975: the area to the east of the river is covered by thick rainforest. There are very few clearings in the forest and not many people live there. To the west of the river, the land is being farmed.

Near Santa Cruz, Bolivia, 2003: just over 25 years later, the forest has disappeared and the land is used for farming. The population of the nearby city has grown from 30,000 to over one million.

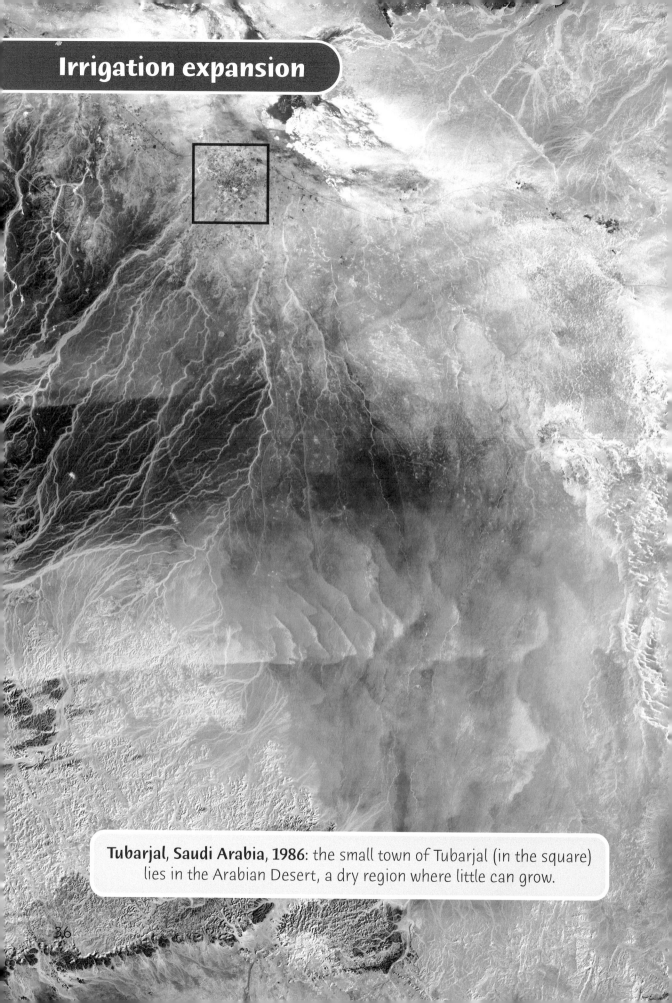

Irrigation expansion

Tubarjal, Saudi Arabia, 1986: the small town of Tubarjal (in the square) lies in the Arabian Desert, a dry region where little can grow.

Tubarjal, Saudi Arabia, 2004: irrigation has transformed the landscape. Each green dot is a field, irrigated by a spinning arm which sprays out water pumped from deep underground. Food production for the town has greatly increased but how long will the water last?

Restoring the landscape

Quarrying for building materials spoils the environment.

This **disused** quarry has been filled with clean water and the landscape has been restored.

Global warming

The most serious environmental problem we face today is global warming. This is the slow and steady rise in the Earth's temperature that is caused by a build-up of carbon dioxide and other gases in the air. These gases are often called "greenhouse gases" because of the effect they are having on the Earth.

Living in a greenhouse

In towns and cities all over the world, power stations, factories, homes and cars all run on oil and coal, which are known as **fossil fuels.** As these fuels are burnt, they release a gas called carbon dioxide, which is building up in the **atmosphere.** The carbon dioxide, along with other gases, traps the Sun's heat in the atmosphere (just as a greenhouse traps heat), instead of allowing it to escape into space. As a result, our world is growing warmer.

how global warming happens

the Sun's rays

Some heat escapes.

Gases in the atmosphere trap heat.

Some heat is trapped.

What are the effects?

Global warming is felt most keenly at the North and South Poles, where temperatures are rising faster than elsewhere. Here, the ice caps are slowly melting. In other cold regions around the world, glaciers – vast rivers of ice – are melting too. All the extra water is causing sea levels to rise, threatening to flood coasts and low-lying islands. Meanwhile, the weather is becoming more extreme. There are more storms and heavy downpours, which cause flooding and other damage. There are more heatwaves and periods of drought, which dry up lakes and turn land into desert.

Polar bears are threatened by global warming.
The icy habitat in which they live is beginning to melt.

Solving the problem

There are no simple solutions to global warming, but, around the world, people are taking steps to cut down the amount of carbon dioxide that is pumped into the air. Scientists are inventing cleaner machines. Natural energy sources, such as sunlight and the wind, are being more widely used. We can all play our part. If we save energy whenever we can, for example by switching off lights and using public transport, each of us can help to improve the situation. That way, slowly but surely, we can repair the damage we've done to the Earth.

Shrinking glaciers

Mount Kilimanjaro, Tanzania, 1974: Kilimanjaro, a dormant volcano, is Africa's highest peak. Although it lies near the equator, the summit is covered by glaciers that formed thousands of years ago.

Mount Kilimanjaro, Tanzania, 2005: in recent years, the glaciers have almost completely vanished. Scientists believe this is the result of global warming.

Tuvalu is a group of low-lying coral islands in the South Pacific. The highest ground is only a few metres above sea level, so global warming and rising seas are a real threat.

At high tide, the islanders' houses are at risk of flooding. The Tuvalese face a worrying future and some of them are leaving the island.

Advancing deserts

In Sahel, Africa, as in many parts of the world, people live on fragile farmland that lies near deserts. Global warming and the destruction of natural vegetation may turn their land into desert.

Shrinking lakes

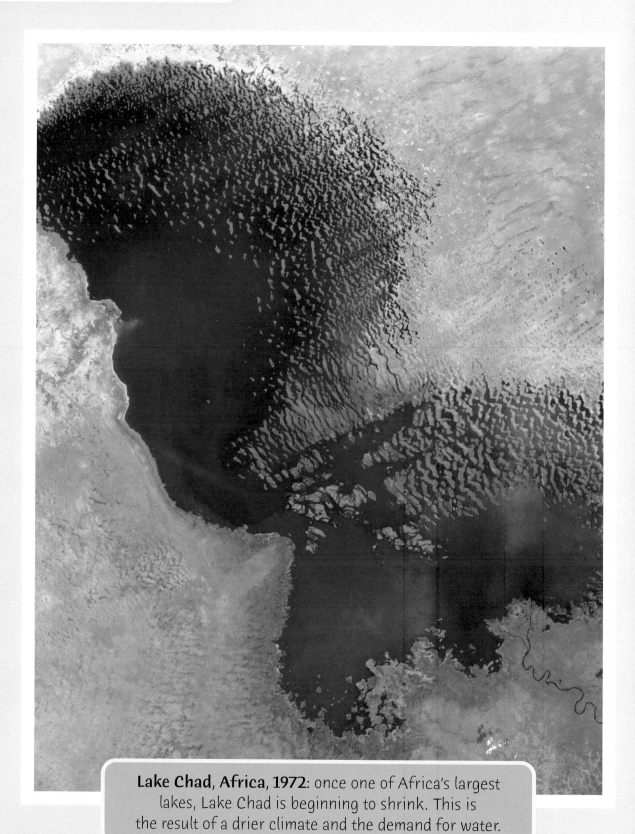

Lake Chad, Africa, 1972: once one of Africa's largest lakes, Lake Chad is beginning to shrink. This is the result of a drier climate and the demand for water.

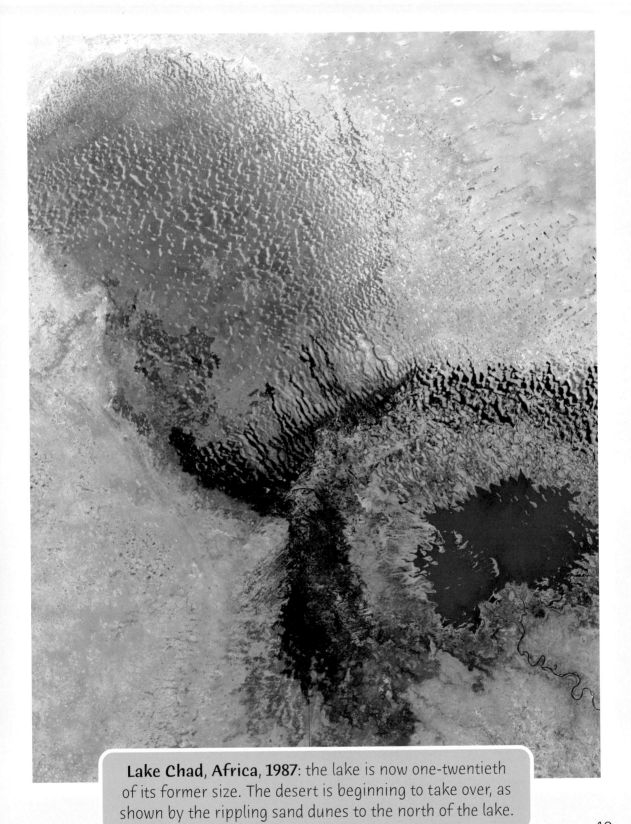

Lake Chad, Africa, 1987: the lake is now one-twentieth of its former size. The desert is beginning to take over, as shown by the rippling sand dunes to the north of the lake.

Observing the Earth

Satellites help us to observe the Earth. Some sit above the same point of the Earth's surface, nearly 36,000 kilometres out into space, keeping pace with the planet as it **rotates**. Others travel around the Earth, about 600 kilometres above the surface, and revisit the same point every two to three weeks. Both kinds of satellite carry **sensors** that gather information about the atmosphere and the surface of the Earth. This is sent to stations on the ground, which collect the signals, interpret the information and pass it on to scientists.

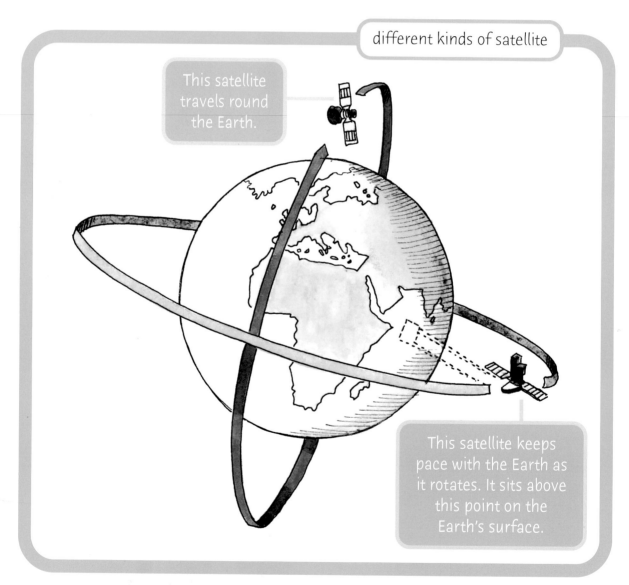

different kinds of satellite

This satellite travels round the Earth.

This satellite keeps pace with the Earth as it rotates. It sits above this point on the Earth's surface.

This sequence of satellite pictures of Venice, Italy, shows just how detailed such images can be.

1 view of Europe

2 view of Italy

3 view of **lagoon** off the Adriatic Sea

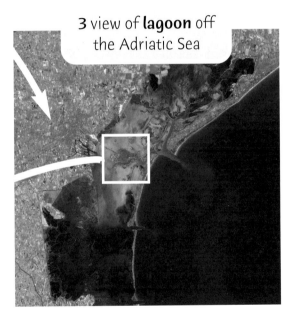

4 view of Venice

5 view of St Mark's Square, Venice

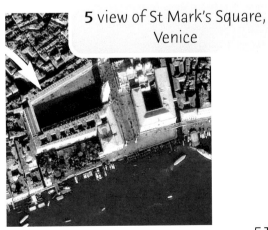

Glossary

atmosphere	the blanket of air that surrounds the Earth
currents	flows of water in one particular direction
debris	the remains of things that have been broken up
disused	not used any more
erodes	wears or rubs away
fossil fuels	natural fuels formed millions of years ago from the remains of living organisms
hemisphere	one half of the Earth
irrigation	the use of dams, sprinklers or channels to water the land in order to help crops to grow in dry places
junks	flat-bottomed sailing boats used in the Far East
lagoon	a large pool of water cut off from the sea by coral reefs or sand bars
minerals	tiny pieces of rock and other solid substances that help to fertilise soil
molten	melted
reservoir	a man-made lake where water is collected and stored
resources	natural materials that can be used by people
rotates	turns or spins around an axis
satellites	machines that orbit the Earth and send back information
sensors	devices that receive a signal and respond to it
submerged	fully covered by water
surge	a sudden rising of the sea

Index

atmosphere   40, 50

carbon dioxide   40, 41

coast   2, 15, 18, 22, 24, 25, 41

deforestation   34, 35

delta   22, 23, 28, 29

desert   31, 36, 37, 41, 46–49

drought   41

Earth's crust   4, 10

Earth's mantle   4, 10

Earth's plates   4, 5, 10, 54, 55

earthquake   2, 4–7, 9, 12

erosion   22–25, 31

farming   23, 26, 27, 34, 35

flood   2, 3, 15–17, 22, 23, 26, 27, 31, 41, 45

glacier   41–43

global warming   3, 40–49

greenhouse gas   40

hurricane   3, 14–17, 54, 55

irrigation   31, 36, 37

lava   10, 11

ocean   2, 4, 5, 9–11, 14, 20–21

pollution   31

population   30, 33, 35

rainforest   30, 34, 35, 54, 55

river   2, 3, 16, 22, 23, 26–29, 31, 34, 35, 41

satellite   3, 5, 8, 15, 16, 21, 26–29, 50, 51

sea   2, 3–5, 14–16, 22, 23, 28, 41, 44, 45, 51

snow   2, 14, 20, 21

Sun   2, 40, 41

tornado   14, 15, 18, 19, 54, 55

tsunami   5, 8, 9

volcano   2, 4, 10–13, 42, 43, 54, 55

water   2, 3, 5, 10, 13–17, 22–29, 30, 31, 37, 41, 48, 49

weather   2, 3, 14–21, 27, 41

Review

Use this map of the world to identify some of the Earth's plates and its continents and oceans. The map also shows where volcanoes and rainforests are found and where tropical storms occur.

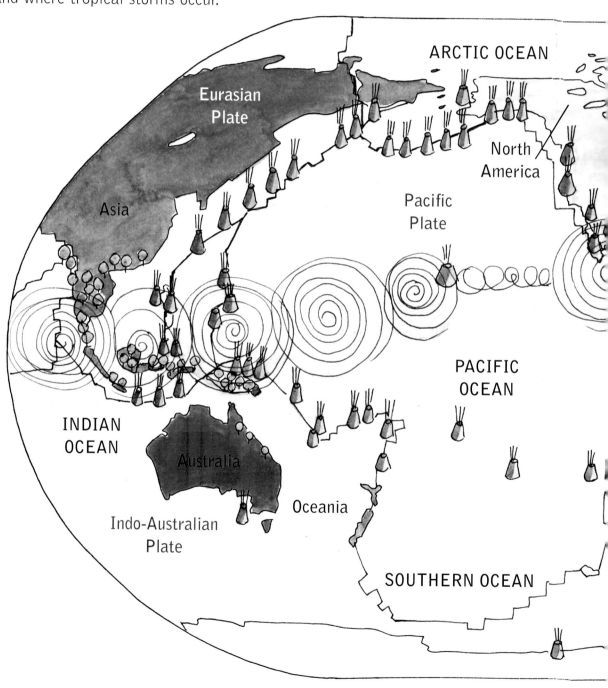

ARCTIC OCEAN

Eurasian Plate

North America

Asia

Pacific Plate

PACIFIC OCEAN

INDIAN OCEAN

Australia

Oceania

Indo-Australian Plate

SOUTHERN OCEAN

Key

the Earth's plates   the Earth's volcanoes

the Earth's rainforests   where tropical storms occur

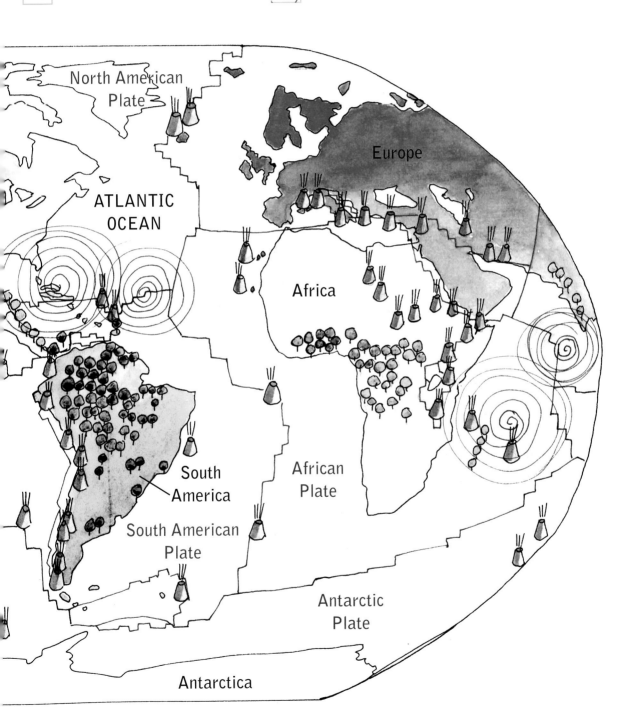

Ideas for reading

Written by Clare Dowdall, PhD
Lecturer and Primary Literacy Consultant

Learning objectives: understand underlying themes, causes and points of view; sustain engagement with longer texts, to make the text come alive; participate in whole-class debate using the conventions and language of debate including standard English

Curriculum links: Geography: Passport to the world

Interest words: atmosphere, current, debris, disused, erodes, hemisphere, irrigation, lagoon, minerals, molten, reservoir, resources, rotates, satellite, sensor, submerged, surge

Resources: ICT, whiteboards, notebooks

Getting started

This book can be read over two or more guided reading sessions.

- Look at the picture on the front cover. Ask children to describe what they can see and what they think is happening (volcano erupting).

- Read the title and the blurb. Discuss what the word "fragile" and the book title "Fragile Earth" might mean. Share children's ideas about how the Earth is changing over time.

- Ask children to think about the author's purpose in writing the book. Will this book be a factual and truthful book or will the author be trying to persuade the reader to share her beliefs about how the Earth is changing?

- Reread the cover and blurb. Discuss how the author has designed the covers to interest and engage readers.

Reading and responding

- Read pp2–3 "Changing Earth" together. Ask children to recall and explain what the author is aiming to do in this book to a partner.

- Discuss the strategies that can be used to help recall information from reading. Remind children about note taking and text highlighting/underlining.

- Model how to make brief notes from pp2–3, and how to use these to formally introduce the book to the children. Remind children to use information from photographs and fact-boxes as well as main text.

- In pairs, ask children to use the contents page to select a topic to research. Ask them to read and make brief notes that will support a formal "Fragile Earth" presentation to a larger group (e.g. the class, school assembly).